Hello and welcome ✈

Traveling can be great fun and in this Airplane activity book you will be able to draw, find, search and color many Airplane themed activities including story based mazes- check out our back page for examples

Grab some colour pencils, a pen, pencil and be excited to complete this activity book.

Activities include
- STORY MAZES
- COLOURING PAGES
- WORD SEARCH
- DESIGN YOUR OWN
- DESIGN CHALLENGES
- MATHS WORKSHEETS
- AND MORE

THIS BOOK BELONGS TO

_____

Quick get to the airport

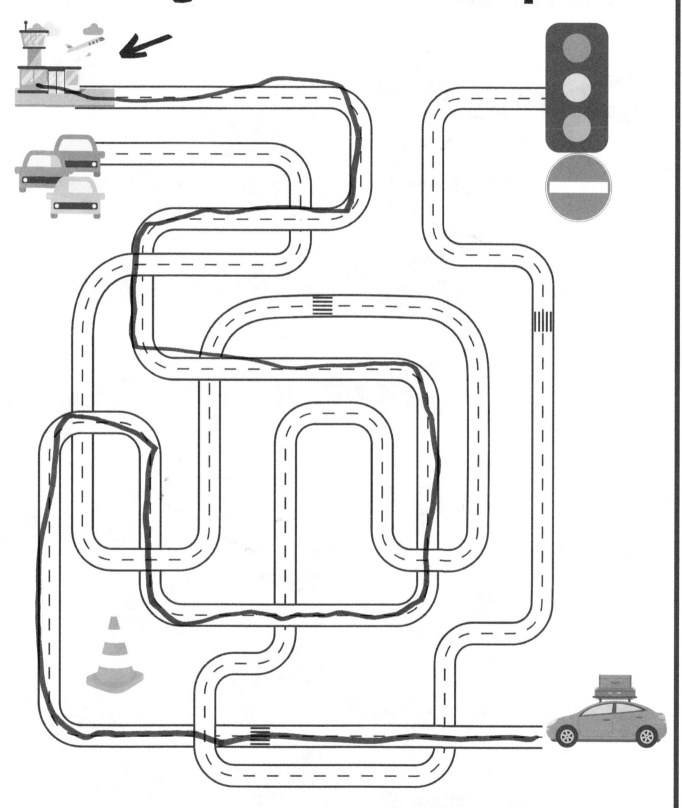

Avoid the car traffic and lights

Find the odd one out

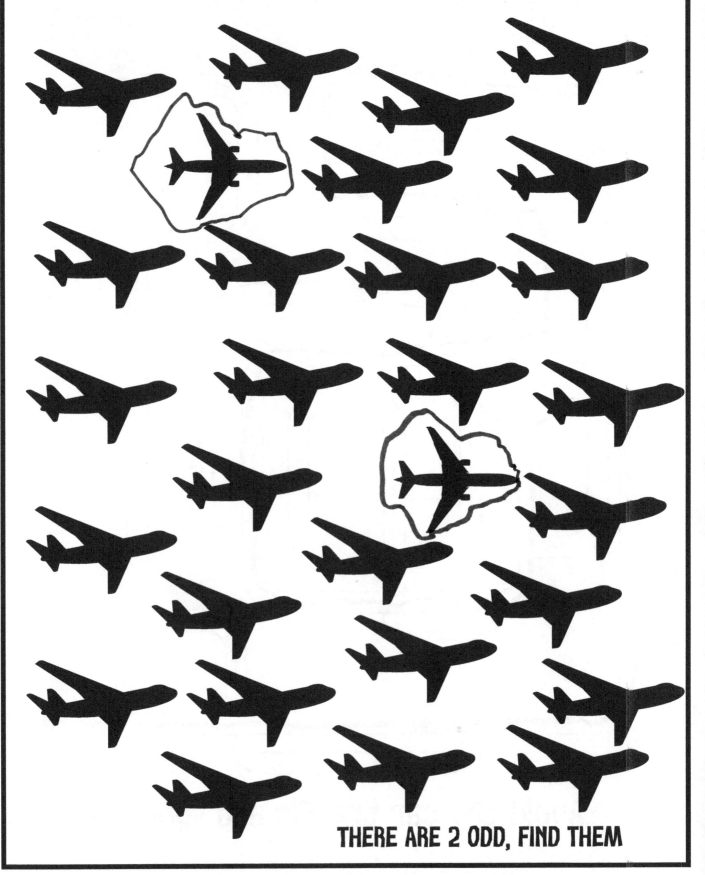

THERE ARE 2 ODD, FIND THEM

Lets go for a swim

Don't forget your float and goggles

Picture Sudoku

This is picture holiday sudoku, put each item in so they appear once in each of the below– Draw them in

row ▦ and column ▦

solutions at the back

Unscramble these words 1

Ask a grown up to help

ENRPLAIA   A _ R P _ _ _ E

NSU   S _ _

ORAITRP   A _ _ P O _ T

ARLXE   R _ L _ X

CEI ARCME   I _ E C _ _ _ _ M

ISMW   S _ _ M

OPLO   P _ _ L

YIMALF   F A _ _ _ Y

IYLDOHA   H _ L _ D _ Y

Some hints are given with words, answers are on the back

Find all the items linked to a holiday

THERE ARE 11 TO FIND

Match the correct planes

Circle the correct number for each item

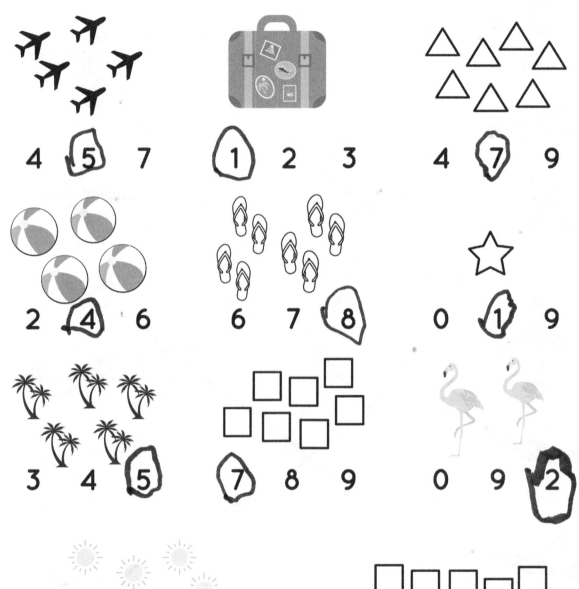

4 (5) 7

(1) 2 3

4 (7) 9

2 (4) 6

6 7 (8)

0 (1) 9

3 4 (5)

(7) 8 9

0 9 (2)

7 (8) 9

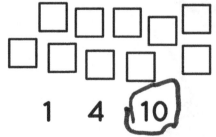

1 4 (10)

Can you find →

Circle all the holiday items

TRAVEL MATCH FUN

In each group there is an object that <u>doesn't</u>
match, can you circle the correct one?

Example

1.

2.

3.

4.

Now try yourself

Draw a group of things where one doesn't belong

Circle what you have seen so far

Plane

Traffic light

Car

Hat

People

Glasses

Suitcase

Can you draw anything else you have seen?

Can you find these words using the words in the box

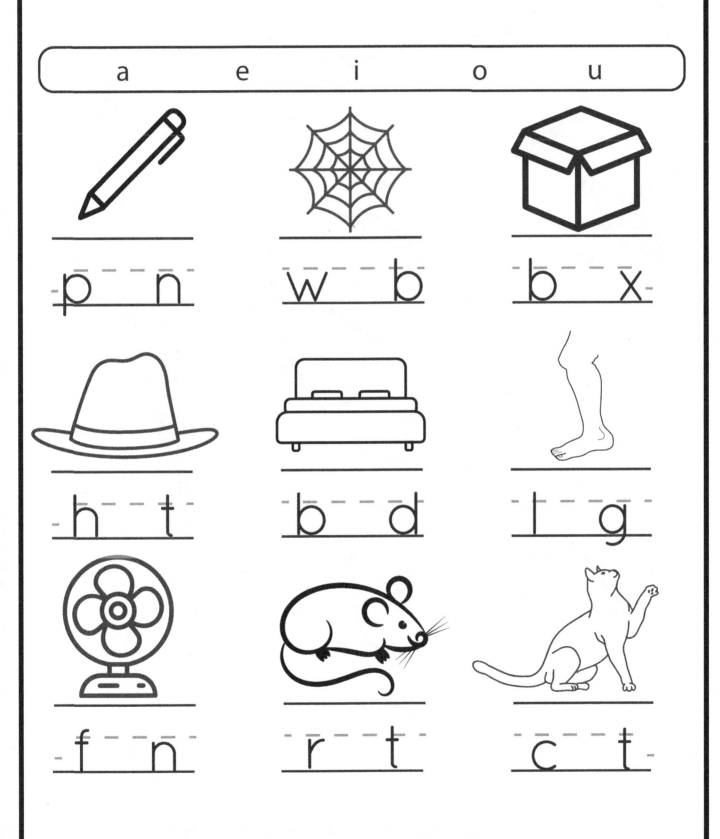

a   e   i   o   u

p _ n

w _ b

b _ x

h _ t

b _ d

l _ g

f _ n

r _ t

c _ t

solution 2

Get to the end and write

where you are going

Collect the passengers for their holiday

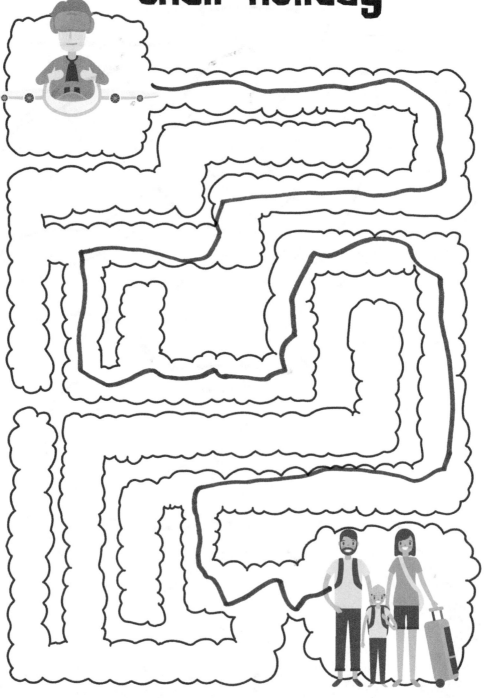

They are excited

How quick can you
get there

Follow the paths
to the planes

Help the pilot land the plane

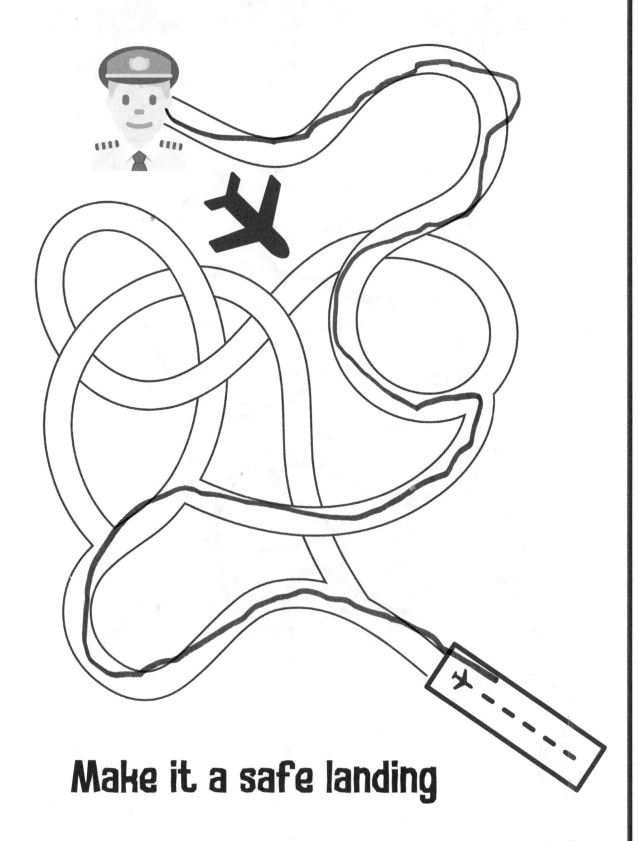

Make it a safe landing

Can you complete the picture of the plane

Color it in too

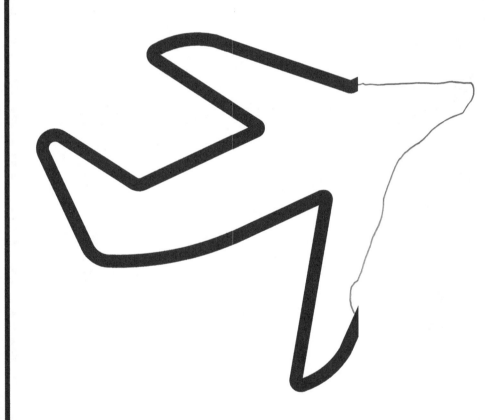

use this to help

Can you complete the picture of the bag
Color it in too

use this to help

Can you complete the picture of the **beachball**
Color it in too

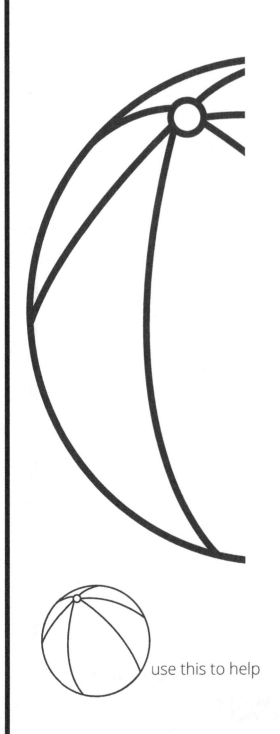

use this to help

In the box below add everything to do with a holiday

Can you draw them?

I LOVE PLANES

PLANES ARE FAST

PLANES MAKE LOUD NOISES

THERE ARE DIFFERENT TYPES
OF PLANES

LETS GO ON HOLIDAY

I'M GOING ON A PLANE

I LIKE LOOKING
OUT THE WINDOW

I'M HUNGRY

CAN YOU TRACE THESE WORDS

Plane

Beach

Ball

Sun

Sand

Hot

Airport

Glasses

Food

Unscramble these words 2

Ask a grown up to help

ECAHB   B _ A _ H

OHLTE   _ _ T _ L

MRSUME   S U _ _ _ R

AGB   _ _ G

NFU   _ U _

OODF   F _ O _

IKNRD   _ R I _ K

AMGES   G _ _ E S

ATH   _ A _

Some hints are given with words, answers are on the back

Airplane Picture Sudoku

Easy

This is airplane picture sudoku, put each item in so they appear once in each of the below draw them in

row ⊞ , column ⊞ , and block ⊞ .

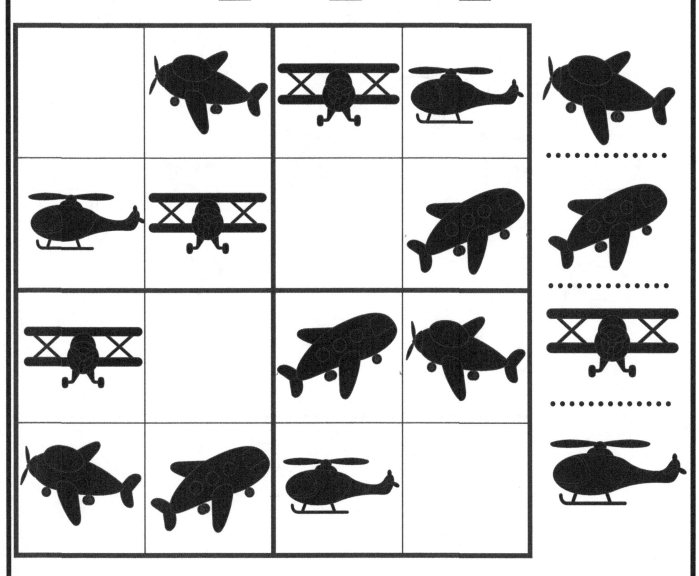

Count how many

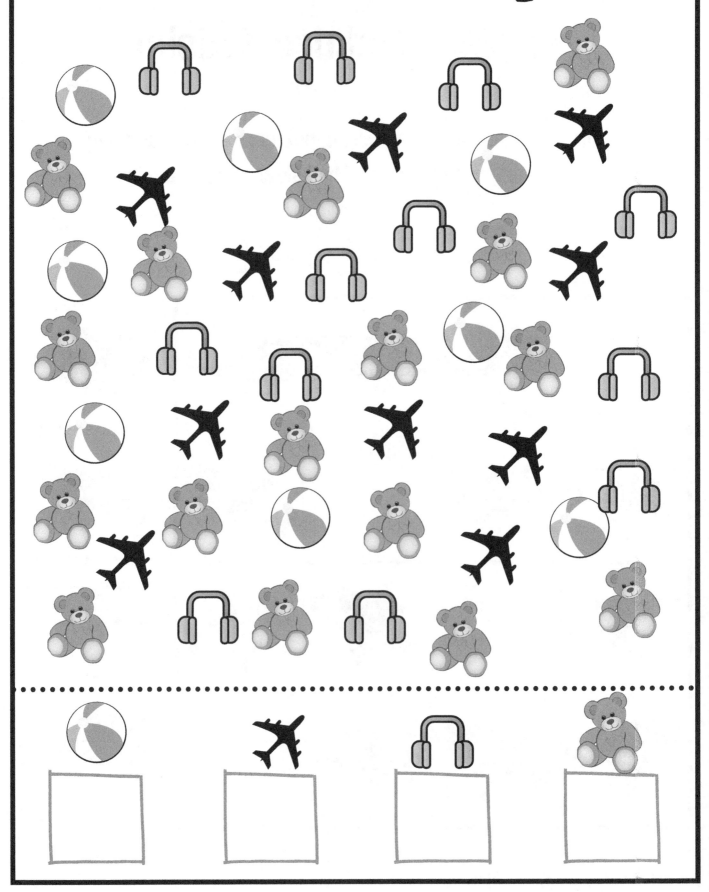

Addition fun

Easy

1)
```
   1
+  8
___
```

2)
```
   6
+  1
___
```

3)
```
   2
+  6
___
```

4)
```
   4
+  5
___
```

5)
```
   8
+  1
___
```

6)
```
   7
+  2
___
```

7)
```
   4
+  1
___
```

8)
```
   1
+  5
___
```

9)
```
   5
+  2
___
```

10)
```
   3
+  6
___
```

11)
```
   2
+  7
___
```

12)
```
   1
+  4
___
```

13)
```
   2
+  3
___
```

14)
```
   3
+  1
___
```

15)
```
   1
+  7
___
```

16)
```
   2
+  4
___
```

17)
```
   1
+  6
___
```

18)
```
   2
+  5
___
```

19)
```
   7
+  1
___
```

20)
```
   6
+  3
___
```

Subtraction fun

1)
$$9 - 2$$

2)
$$5 - 1$$

3)
$$4 - 1$$

4)
$$9 - 7$$

5)
$$4 - 2$$

6)
$$2 - 1$$

7)
$$6 - 5$$

8)
$$9 - 6$$

9)
$$7 - 5$$

10)
$$7 - 2$$

11)
$$9 - 4$$

12)
$$8 - 4$$

13)
$$5 - 4$$

14)
$$8 - 5$$

15)
$$8 - 1$$

16)
$$5 - 3$$

17)
$$7 - 3$$

18)
$$8 - 2$$

19)
$$8 - 7$$

20)
$$7 - 1$$

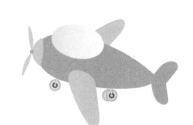

Addition fun

1)
```
   46
 + 43
 ____
```

2)
```
   33
 + 53
 ____
```

3)
```
   11
 + 28
 ____
```

4)
```
   15
 + 81
 ____
```

5)
```
   12
 + 37
 ____
```

6)
```
   68
 + 10
 ____
```

7)
```
   36
 + 23
 ____
```

8)
```
   40
 + 44
 ____
```

9)
```
   13
 + 73
 ____
```

10)
```
   63
 + 14
 ____
```

11)
```
   20
 + 57
 ____
```

12)
```
   30
 + 31
 ____
```

13)
```
   59
 + 30
 ____
```

14)
```
   18
 + 51
 ____
```

15)
```
   40
 + 11
 ____
```

16)
```
   31
 + 45
 ____
```

17)
```
   30
 + 60
 ____
```

18)
```
   44
 + 44
 ____
```

19)
```
   32
 + 27
 ____
```

20)
```
   31
 + 51
 ____
```

Subtraction fun

1)
```
  85
- 21
```

2)
```
  74
- 50
```

3)
```
  98
- 40
```

4)
```
  67
- 10
```

5)
```
  39
- 23
```

6)
```
  83
- 20
```

7)
```
  58
- 10
```

8)
```
  65
- 44
```

9)
```
  67
- 35
```

10)
```
  89
- 21
```

11)
```
  25
- 10
```

12)
```
  82
- 10
```

13)
```
  98
- 47
```

14)
```
  89
- 17
```

15)
```
  39
- 26
```

16)
```
  98
- 11
```

17)
```
  88
- 14
```

18)
```
  86
- 40
```

19)
```
  92
- 71
```

20)
```
  99
- 87
```

Picture Word Search

```
Q S I F U U A B A E
Y A Z R M X I A I F
B N I W B D B L R T
I D C B R B Q L P B
K A E G E M R C L A
U L C D L A O V A G
G S R Z L B C H N I
H X E B A V Q H E K
M U A V M V S U N C
R F M T T U J V A L
```

Umbrella

Bag

Sun

Airplane

Sandals

Ice cream

Beach

Ball

Answers on the back

Airplane words

R S G I O V F S G C

T S L E E P L I T Z

K L F L Y E I Z T M

J U X V E X T Q I G

M S O H I O S O C D

L C W L L S E W K K

D A Y I H H A H E W

I B P L Q G T X T C

V I P L A N E H Z M

Z N K V Q N I H V N

FLY
WHEELS
PILOT
SLEEP

SEAT
CABIN
PLANE
TICKET

Find the Airplane words

```
X  P  X  G  X  D  P  Y  E  R
U  J  B  E  L  T  O  L  I  K
M  N  T  Y  D  A  S  O  K  Y
P  U  A  E  W  I  N  G  R  Z
U  E  E  N  A  J  J  I  H  T
B  P  F  M  C  S  S  G  H  T
S  X  W  J  Q  K  D  G  M  U
G  A  J  P  Z  Y  I  D  I  T
C  V  B  A  W  L  O  D  L  G
D  R  U  N  W  A  Y  E  A  T
```

AISLE

DOOR

RUNWAY

SPEED

BELT

LIGHT

SKY

WING

Its holiday time

L U E B M F H A T L
F Y F Q H D S X A E
Y S X E I I O L X E
B Z N S O J C Q I H
E Q D U H J J E W O
A Y R N R X V B A T
C W D A U L M X Q E
H I C W A V E S T L
I H Z N N Y I E T L
Q F R O O F B V A Y

BEACH   CAR
HAT   HOTEL
ICE   SUN
TAXI   WAVES

Vacation food words

```
B  F  W  S  D  U  D  X  H  I
S  L  C  U  E  B  P  R  R  O
P  E  W  M  S  A  D  F  L  U
O  Y  H  M  S  R  R  R  E  M
R  W  E  E  E  B  I  U  R  Z
T  R  E  R  R  E  N  I  M  U
S  X  P  Z  T  Q  K  T  L  P
T  F  O  O  D  U  S  J  M  R
C  G  W  W  I  E  Y  A  Q  X
M  C  E  O  J  M  C  Y  X  C
```

BARBEQUE
DESSERT
FOOD
SPORTS

CAMP
DRINKS
FRUIT
SUMMER

Find the colors

```
H  D  N  U  X  U  E  E  A  L
A  D  E  E  E  Q  H  S  R  O
M  O  N  Z  Z  E  D  E  B  Q
Y  R  P  D  Y  E  T  R  Z  L
X  A  I  U  R  I  K  M  F  B
D  N  N  X  H  O  D  C  A  L
M  G  K  W  G  R  E  E  N  A
A  E  N  N  P  T  M  X  K  C
S  S  B  Y  E  L  L  O  W  K
Z  A  B  L  U  E  X  P  K  A
```

BLACK
GREEN
PINK
WHITE

BLUE
ORANGE
RED
YELLOW

Holiday sports

```
P  P  S  W  T  P  I  X  M  U
L  C  Q  J  J  E  O  S  M  F
E  T  W  C  O  K  N  O  F  O
Z  R  U  N  N  I  N  G  L  O
M  B  A  S  E  B  A  L  L  T
H  C  Z  Q  A  V  S  V  O  B
U  R  T  X  C  L  I  M  B  A
J  J  E  T  S  K  I  O  P  L
Z  T  N  H  N  S  W  I  M  L
L  W  N  V  N  A  D  R  T  L
```

BASEBALL
CLIMB
JETSKI
RUNNING

CANOE
FOOTBALL
POOL
SWIM

Time for the beach

B	W	M	Y	A	E	Z	Q	W	N
U	C	L	O	K	H	K	V	U	Y
C	X	A	A	L	X	T	F	C	H
K	P	C	N	G	R	E	L	A	X
E	S	S	S	D	U	F	Z	Z	O
T	W	A	W	P	Y	P	K	B	Y
I	B	N	G	A	A	X	N	D	B
Z	T	D	Q	G	R	D	W	Z	Q
Z	N	O	U	Z	H	M	E	G	Q
F	X	A	X	D	F	B	S	R	A

BUCKET
CANDY
RELAX
SPADE

CAKE
FUN
SAND
WARM

Complete the maze

Help the boy get to his beach ball

Can you get to the end?

Lets build a
sandcastle

Take the bucket and spade to make
a bigger sandcastle

Get to the end of the maze

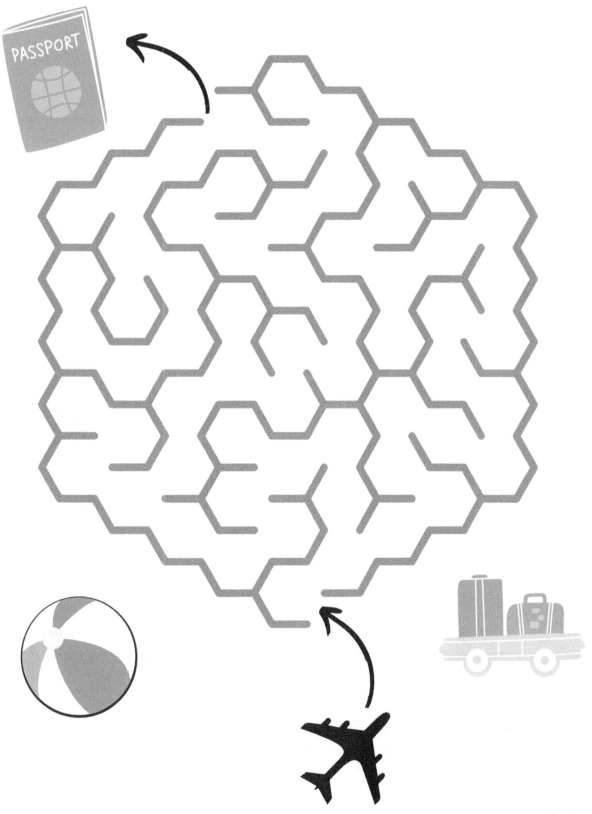

Can you get to the departures

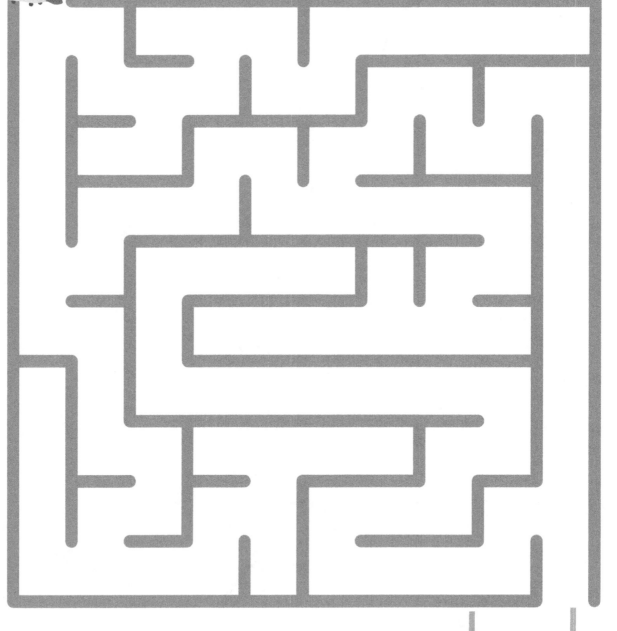

Ready to fly

DEPARTURES

Can you guide the plane to the runway?

 # TIC TAC TOE

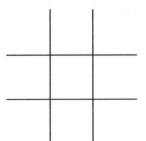 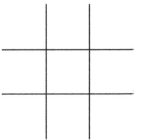

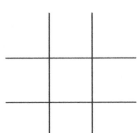

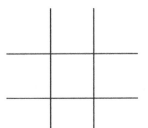 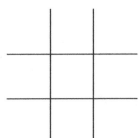

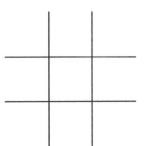 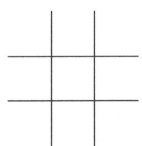

Winner _____

 # TIC TAC TOE

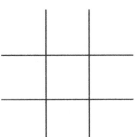 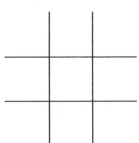 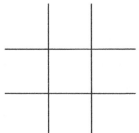

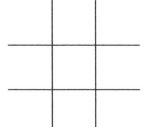 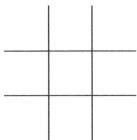

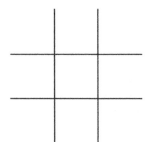 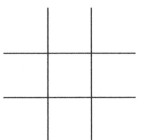

Winner _____

 # TIC TAC TOE

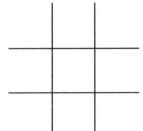

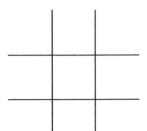

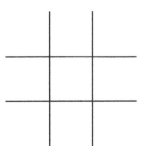

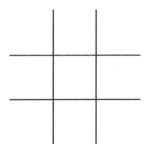

Winner _____

Solutions

If you need them

Picture Sudoku (solution)

This is picture holiday sudoku, put each item in so they appear once in each of the below– Draw them in

Medium

row ▦ and column ▦

Airplane Picture Sudoku
Solution

This is airplane picture sudoku, put each item in so they appear once in each of the below draw and COLOR THEM IN

row ⊞ , column ⊞ , and block ⊞ .

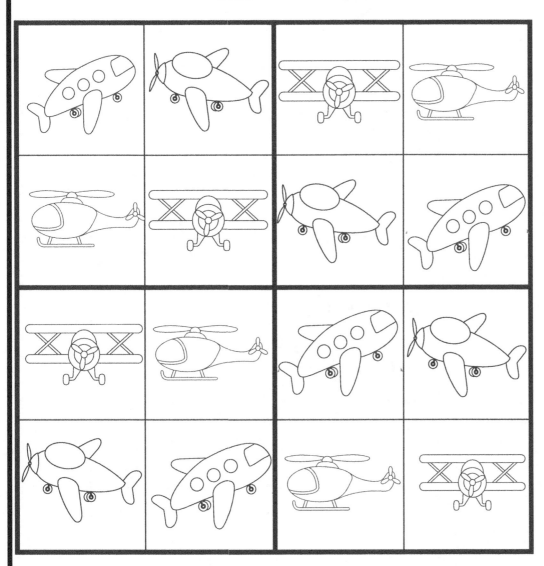

Can you find these words using the words in the box (solutions)

a   e   i   o   u

pen   web   box

hat   bed   leg

fan   rat   cat

AIRPLANE WORD SCRAMBLE

ENRPLAIA	AIRPLANE
NSU	SUN
ORAITRP	AIRPORT
ARLXE	RELAX
CEI ARCME	ICE CREAM
ISMW	SWIM
OPLO	POOL
YIMALF	FAMILY
IYLDOHA	HOLIDAY

AIRPLANE WORD SCRAMBLE 2

ECAHB	BEACH
OHLTE	HOTEL
MRSUME	SUMMER
AGB	BAG
NFU	FUN
OODF	FOOD
IKNRD	DRINK
AMGES	GAMES
ATH	HAT

count how many solution

8   10   12   16

picture wordsearch solution

```
Q S I F U U A B A E
Y A Z R M X I A I F
B N I W B D B L R T
I D C B R B Q L P B
K A E G E M R C L A
U L C D L A O V A G
G S R Z L B C H N I
H X E B A V Q H E K
M U A V M V S U N C
R F M T T U J V A L
```

Umbrella   Ice cream   Beach   Ball   Sun   Airplane

Sandals   Bag

TRAVEL MATCH FUN (SOLUTION)

In each group there is an object that doesn't match, can you circle the correct one?

Example

1.

2.

3.

4.

Now try yourself

Draw a group of things where one doesn't belong

Match the correct planes
solutions

solution 1

solution 2

Shaped maze solutions

solution 3

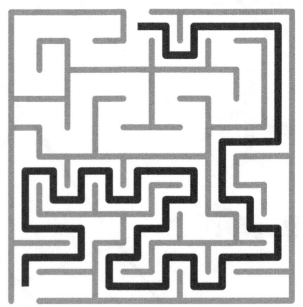

solution 4

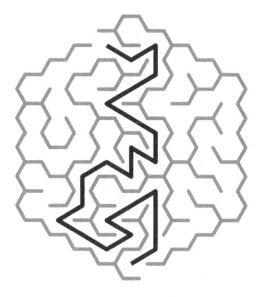

solution 5

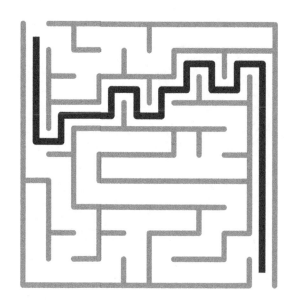

solution 6

Shaped maze solutions

solution 7

solution 1

solution 2

Themed maze solutions

solution 3

solution 4

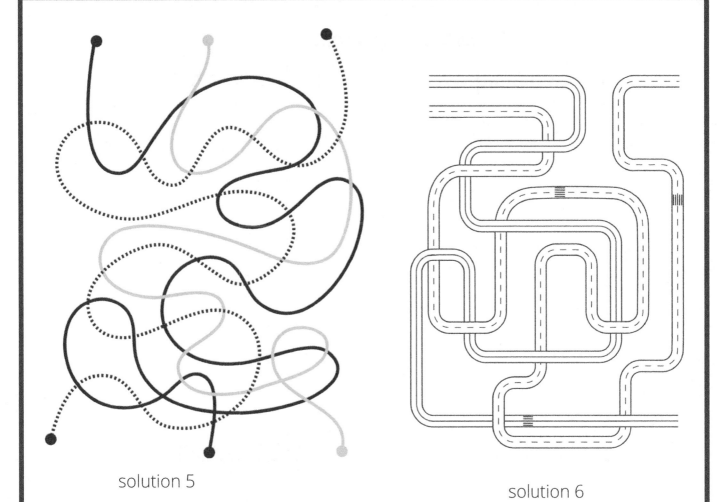

solution 5

solution 6

Themed maze solutions

solution 7

Math solutions

Addition Easy

1)
```
    1
+   8
―――――
    9
```
2)
```
    6
+   1
―――――
    7
```
3)
```
    2
+   6
―――――
    8
```
4)
```
    4
+   5
―――――
    9
```

5)
```
    8
+   1
―――――
    9
```
6)
```
    7
+   2
―――――
    9
```
7)
```
    4
+   1
―――――
    5
```
8)
```
    1
+   5
―――――
    6
```

9)
```
    5
+   2
―――――
    7
```
10)
```
    3
+   6
―――――
    9
```
11)
```
    2
+   7
―――――
    9
```
12)
```
    1
+   4
―――――
    5
```

13)
```
    2
+   3
―――――
    5
```
14)
```
    3
+   1
―――――
    4
```
15)
```
    1
+   7
―――――
    8
```
16)
```
    2
+   4
―――――
    6
```

17)
```
    1
+   6
―――――
    7
```
18)
```
    2
+   5
―――――
    7
```
19)
```
    7
+   1
―――――
    8
```
20)
```
    6
+   3
―――――
    9
```

Addition Hard

1)
```
   46
+  43
―――――
   89
```
2)
```
   33
+  53
―――――
   86
```
3)
```
   11
+  28
―――――
   39
```
4)
```
   15
+  81
―――――
   96
```

5)
```
   12
+  37
―――――
   49
```
6)
```
   68
+  10
―――――
   78
```
7)
```
   36
+  23
―――――
   59
```
8)
```
   40
+  44
―――――
   84
```

9)
```
   13
+  73
―――――
   86
```
10)
```
   63
+  14
―――――
   77
```
11)
```
   20
+  57
―――――
   77
```
12)
```
   30
+  31
―――――
   61
```

13)
```
   59
+  30
―――――
   89
```
14)
```
   18
+  51
―――――
   69
```
15)
```
   40
+  11
―――――
   51
```
16)
```
   31
+  45
―――――
   76
```

17)
```
   30
+  60
―――――
   90
```
18)
```
   44
+  44
―――――
   88
```
19)
```
   32
+  27
―――――
   59
```
20)
```
   31
+  51
―――――
   82
```

Subtraction Easy

1)
```
    9
-   2
―――――
    7
```
2)
```
    5
-   1
―――――
    4
```
3)
```
    4
-   1
―――――
    3
```
4)
```
    9
-   7
―――――
    2
```

5)
```
    4
-   2
―――――
    2
```
6)
```
    2
-   1
―――――
    1
```
7)
```
    6
-   5
―――――
    1
```
8)
```
    9
-   6
―――――
    3
```

9)
```
    7
-   5
―――――
    2
```
10)
```
    7
-   2
―――――
    5
```
11)
```
    9
-   4
―――――
    5
```
12)
```
    8
-   4
―――――
    4
```

13)
```
    5
-   4
―――――
    1
```
14)
```
    8
-   5
―――――
    3
```
15)
```
    8
-   1
―――――
    7
```
16)
```
    5
-   3
―――――
    2
```

17)
```
    7
-   3
―――――
    4
```
18)
```
    8
-   2
―――――
    6
```
19)
```
    8
-   7
―――――
    1
```
20)
```
    7
-   1
―――――
    6
```

Subtraction Hard

1)
```
   85
-  21
―――――
   64
```
2)
```
   74
-  50
―――――
   24
```
3)
```
   98
-  40
―――――
   58
```
4)
```
   67
-  10
―――――
   57
```

5)
```
   39
-  23
―――――
   16
```
6)
```
   83
-  20
―――――
   63
```
7)
```
   58
-  10
―――――
   48
```
8)
```
   65
-  44
―――――
   21
```

9)
```
   67
-  35
―――――
   32
```
10)
```
   89
-  21
―――――
   68
```
11)
```
   25
-  10
―――――
   15
```
12)
```
   82
-  10
―――――
   72
```

13)
```
   98
-  47
―――――
   51
```
14)
```
   89
-  17
―――――
   72
```
15)
```
   39
-  26
―――――
   13
```
16)
```
   98
-  11
―――――
   87
```

17)
```
   88
-  14
―――――
   74
```
18)
```
   86
-  40
―――――
   46
```
19)
```
   92
-  71
―――――
   21
```
20)
```
   99
-  87
―――――
   12
```

Airplane words

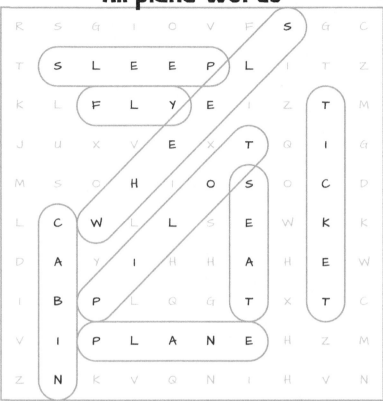

Find the Airplane words

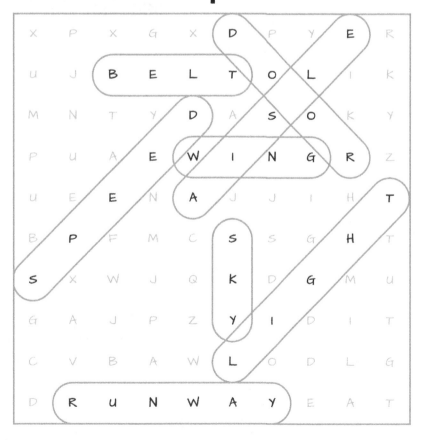

its holiday time

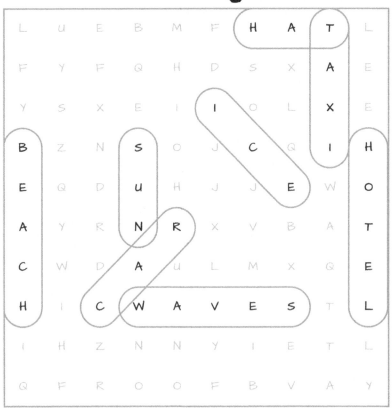

vacation food words

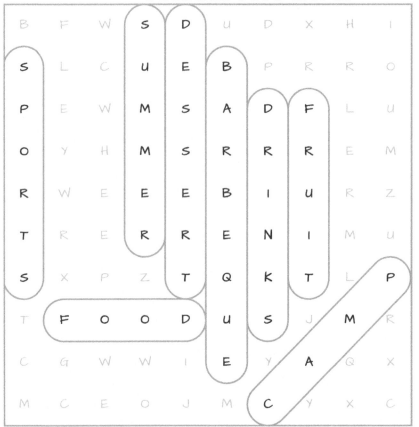

Find the colors

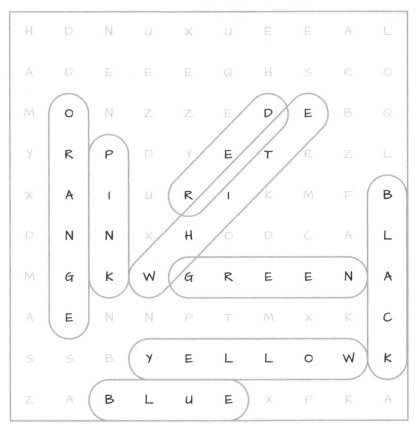

holiday sports

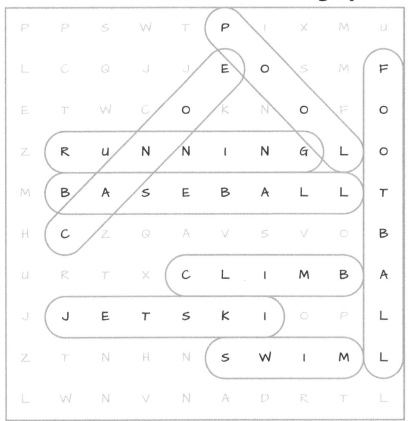

Time for the beach

B	W	M	Y	A	E	Z	Q	W	N
u		C	L	O	K	H	K	V	u	Y
C	X	A	A	L	X	T	F	C	H
K	P	C	N	G	R	E	L	A	X
E	S	S	S	D	U	F	Z	Z	O
T	W	A	W	P	Y	P	K	B	Y
i	B	N	G	A	A	X	N	D	B
Z	T	D	Q	G	R	D	W	Z	Q
Z	N	O	U	Z	H	M	E	G	Q
F	X	A	X	D	F	B	S	R	A